THE FOKKER Dr.1 & D VII
IN WORLD WAR I

Heinz J. Nowarra

SCHIFFER MILITARY HISTORY

West Chester, PA

Sources: Nowarra archives

Translated from the German by Don Cox.

Copyright © 1991 by Schiffer Publishing Ltd.
Library of Congress Catalog Number: 91-62743.

Printed in the United States of America.
ISBN: 0-88740-353-0

This title was originally published under the title,
Richthofen's Dreidekker,
by Podzun-Pallas Verlag, Friedberg.

We are interested in hearing from authors with book ideas on related topics. We are also looking for good photographs in the military history area. We will copy your photos and credit you should your materials be used in a future Schiffer project.

Published by Schiffer Publishing, Ltd.
1469 Morstein Road
West Chester, Pennsylvania 19380
Please write for a free catalog.
This book may be purchased from the publisher.
Please include $2.00 postage.
Try your bookstore first.

The brothers Manfred (right) and Lothar von Richthofen during the spring of 1918.

The Fokker Triplane and its Successor

This photojournal of the two most famous German fighters of World War I is the result of years of research by the author. All the information and pictures presented here come from former members of the Albatros and Fokker Works, as well as from former members of *Jagdgeschwader* 1 and 2; details of the aircraft themselves were mostly provided by the test pilots Erich Kuhlisch and Richard Scholz, as well as the Albatros design engineer Willi Hackenberger.

As the leader of the 1st *Jagdgeschwader* of Germany and the most successful fighter pilot of the First World War, *Rittmeister* Manfred Freiherr von Richthofen has become a legendary figure. And in connection with his name, his Fokker triplane has become almost as legendary. It's not clear why, since 57 of Richthofen's 80 victories (or almost 75%) were achieved in other aircraft types, mostly Albatros. Taking a look at the development of the triplane, it can be seen that in reality it was an aircraft plagued with many problems.

The German *Jagdwaffe* enjoyed aerial superiority over its English counterpart in April, 1917. It was during this time that Sopwith introduced a triplane which was markedly superior to the best German fighter of the day, the Albatros D III. This English triplane was only flown by pilots of the

Hauptmann Wilberg (left), greets Manfred von Richthofen during the Kaiser's review of the troops in August of 1917 in Flanders.

Above: This was the first Sopwith triplane to be forced down by a German *Jagdstaffel*. In the background can be seen the Albatros D Va aircraft of this *Staffel*.

Naval "A" Fighting Squadron. One of these aircraft was forced to land behind the German lines in an almost undamaged state and was presented for study to the German aircraft manufacturers in Adlershof. To a man, these manufacturers immediately began working on their own triplane designs. Only Antony Fokker, a Dutch-born German resident, and his coworker Reinhold Platz, succeeded in designing an aircraft that was better than its British model. The first test aircraft (V.3), a cantilever triplane with a 100hp Oberursel engine, was rolled out at the beginning of May. Due to poor stability, a somewhat more stabile V.4 triplane with a 110hp Oberursel was built, and as the first aircraft of the series received the designation F I/101/17. This aircraft was used for all test flights, and two additional F I planes (102/17 and 103/17) were completed. That summer two other designs were also completed: the V.5 with a Goebel 160hp engine and the V.6 with a Mercedes 160hp. In order to provide an even greater boost in performance, Fokker constructed a tri- plus biplane, the V.8 — which was a failure — and the V.10 triplane with a Siemens Sh 3 engine and four-blade propeller.

On July 1, 1917, *Jagdgeschwader* I was formed from the *Jagdstaffeln*, or *Jasta*, Nrs. 4, 6, 10, and 11, and Manfred von Richthofen, who was the leader of *Jasta* 11, was appointed as the commander of this new unit. However, only six days later Richthofen was seriously wounded. On July 21, he travelled from the

Left: This Sopwith triplane was brought down by *Leutnant* Mohnicke of *Jasta* 11 on July 11th, 1917 near Comines. This was *Lt.* Mohnicke's third aerial victory.

Fokker's first experimental triplane, the V.3, with a 100hp Oberursel engine.

The provisional final design of the triplane: V.4 (F I/101/17) with Le Rhône or Oberursel 110hp engine.

The Fokker V.6, a larger V.4 with a 120hp Mercedes engine.

Fokker hoped to achieve even greater climb performance with this quintuplane. Engine: Mercedes 120hp.

Fokker (wearing flight cap) and his chief engineer Reinhold Platz during final assembly of F I/102/17.

Above: Manfred von Richthofen, the "Red Baron" (left) with an officer of *Jasta* 11. In the background is F I/102/17, with which he achieved his 60th aerial victory on 1 September 1917.

Below is the red triplane, Dr. I 152/17, which Richthofen used to achieve his 66th aerial victory and which was later put on display in the Berlin Zeughaus. In 1944 it became a victim of an American bombing raid.

Above: Manfred von Richthofen in his F I/102/17 at the beginning of September 1917.

Below is Dr. I 425/17 in which the Red Baron took off from Cappy on an enemy patrol, never to return.

Fokker Dr. I 154/17 in Schwerin-Görries prior to deliver to its unit.

hospital in Kortrijk to pay a visit to his *Geschwader*. He took this opportunity to announce: "You'll be getting Fokker triplanes, (then) you'll climb like monkeys and be as maneuverable as the devil." He again assumed command of *JG* 1 on July 25. On July 30, *Jasta* 10 was assigned a new leader in the person of *Leutnant* Werner Voss. He and Richthofen were to be the first ones to fly the triplane operationally. But it was to be five more weeks before they were able to do so. It was on 1 September that F I/102/17 was finally delivered to the unit, and was immediately put through its paces by Richthofen. On 3 September Richthofen entered the following evaluation in the *Geschwader* logbook: "F I/102/17 is superior to all foes." Then Richthofen was ordered to go on leave. On 15 September he received the news at home that *Leutnant* Kurt Wolff had been shot down while flying F I/102/17. Thus began the streak of misfortune for the triplane, which had now received the designation of Dr. I for series-produced aircraft. F I/103/17 was given to *Leutnant* Voss. He was shot down on 24 September. On the 27th of September *Leutnant* Müller of *Jasta* 11 plummeted to his death while test flying a triplane. Three days later Richthofen himself totally destroyed Dr. I/114/17. On the same day *Leutnant* Gontermann, the leader of *Jasta* 15, crashed when the wings broke away on Dr. I/115/17, and the next day the same thing happened to *Lt.* Pastor of *Jasta* 11 in Dr. I/121/17. On November 6, *Leutnant* Löwenhardt of *Jasta* 10 also was a victim of wing structure failure. The triplane was then pulled out of service and Fokker installed strengtheners in the wings. These improved Dr. 1 aircraft arrived at the front beginning in February.

The Austrian successor to the throne, Otto von Habsburg (5th from left), during a visit to *Jasta* 10 in July of 1917. Continuing from the left: (2nd) *Lt.* Werner Voss, (3rd) *Major* Siegert of Idflieg, (7th) *Hptm.* Wilberg, (9th) *Oblt.* von Döring, and finally *Oblt.* Bodenschatz. These last three individuals held leadership positions in the Luftwaffe from 1933-1945.

Lt. Werner Voss, leader of *Jasta* 10, in front of his "Silver Triplane."

Lt. Gontermann, leader of *Jasta* 15, with Fokker Dr. I 115/17.

Gontermann's fatal crash involving Dr. I 115/117, following his 39th victory on 30 October 1917.

Voss' successor: *Oberlt*, Erich Löwenhardt, killed on 10 August 1918 after 53 victories.

Fokker V.10 with a Siemens and Halske Sh III 160hp engine, which took part in the fly-off in January 1918.

Jagdstaffel 26 of *Jagdgeschwader* 3. Posing in front of the first triplane is *Offizierstellvertreter* Otto Esswein, killed on 21 July 1918 after 12 victories.

Right: Fokker Dr. I of *Jasta* 26 is pushed into a parking area after landing. The *Staffel* was based in Sissone (France) in the summer of 1918.

Left: A few other triplanes of *Jasta* 26 in Sissone. This is the *Staffel* to which Bruno Loerzer belonged, who later went on to command *Jagdgeschwader* 3 as a Luftwaffe general.

Left: *Hauptmann* Adolf Ritter von Tutscheck, commander of *Jagdgeschwader* 2, with his Fokker Dr. I 404/17 in which he perished on 15 March 1918 with 27 victories.

Right: *Oberleutnant* Hermann Göring, the future *Reichsmarschall* and, from 6 July 1918 onward, Richthofen's successor as leader of *Jagdgeschwader* 1.

Right: *Leutnant* Rudolf Stark, the last leader of the Bavarian *Jagdstaffel* 35, seen here in the summer of 1918 in Epinoy.

Left: *Leutnant* von Raben, *Jasta* 7, was forced down by French fighters in 1918 and became a prisoner of war.

15

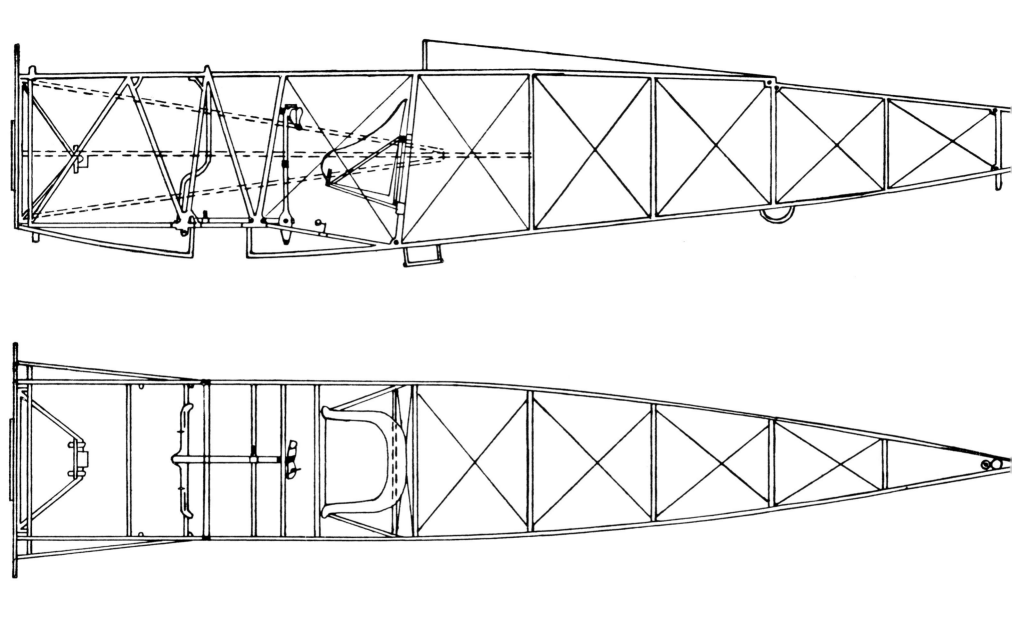

Factory drawings of the Fokker Dr. I's fuselage construction.

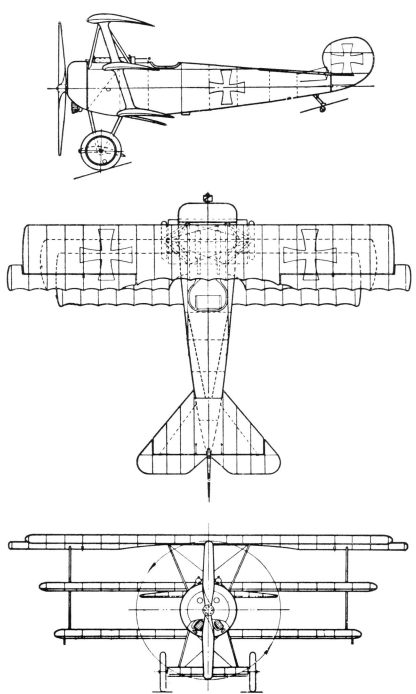

Three-view drawing of the Fokker Dr. I.

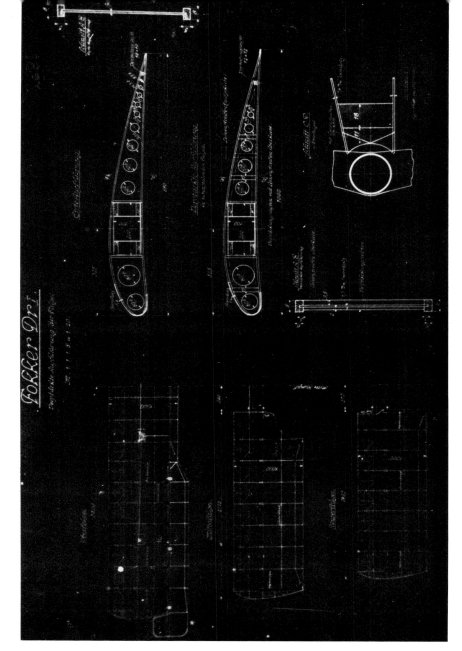

Factory drawings showing the strengthened wing construction on the Fokker Dr. I.

Reproductions of Fokker triplanes as they appeared in the 1933 German film "D III 88."

FOKKER D VII

Captured German aircraft were often used in American films such as "Hell's Angels" and "Dawn Patrol." However, as this picture illustrates, the paint schemes were seldom accurate. This is a Fokker D VII from "Hell's Angels."

Factory pilot and mechanics pose in front of the first design of the Fokker V.11.

Second design of the V.11.

The triplane appeared to hold little joy for those who flew it. This stemmed in part from the fact that the triplane was too slow. Fokker himself said, "The triplane climbed so well that no one noticed how slow it was." So the Fokker team had been working on a new fighter since the autumn of 1917. The Inspection der Fliegertruppen (IdFlieg) did not want to have those pilots stationed in Germany evaluating new aircraft, so it held its first fighter aircraft competition in January of 1918 — to which the best fighter pilots from the front were invited to test the new models. Fokker wanted to demonstrate as many different types as possible, and therefore provided the competition with a few low-wing monoplanes: V.17, V.20, and V.23, two biplanes with rotary engines: V.9 and V.13, as well as the V.11 and V.18 biplanes.

Even Richthofen appeared at this competition and flew V.11 on January 23. He wasn't satisfied with its flight characteristics and demanded several changes. During the testing of V.18 Fokker, who always flew his own aircraft, noticed that the wing dihedral wasn't correct and that the horizontal stabilizers were too small. The aircraft was certainly fast had climbed well, but it was unstable and had a tendency to spin. As Fokker put it, this was an aircraft that could break one's neck. The trials were to officially begin on Monday. Throughout Saturday night and into Sunday morning, Fokker himself, along with two welders, worked on V.18, lengthening its fuselage, changing the wings, and enlarging the horizontal stabilizers. Their success was remarkable. This aircraft, which was to enter production as the Fokker D VII, beat every comer. Fokker was awarded an initial contract for 400 aircraft at

The Fokker V.18 seen during the fly-off in Adlershof during January of 1918.

Fokker V.21 with 160hp Mercedes, early 1918.

Fokker V.22, engine is probably the 185hp Austro-Daimler.

Fokker V.24 with a 220hp Benz Bz IV, spring 1918.

A factory-fresh Fokker D VII 507/18 with a 185hp BMW III, shown here in the spring of 1918.

Fokker D VII 461/18 seen during the 1918 trials in Adlershof.

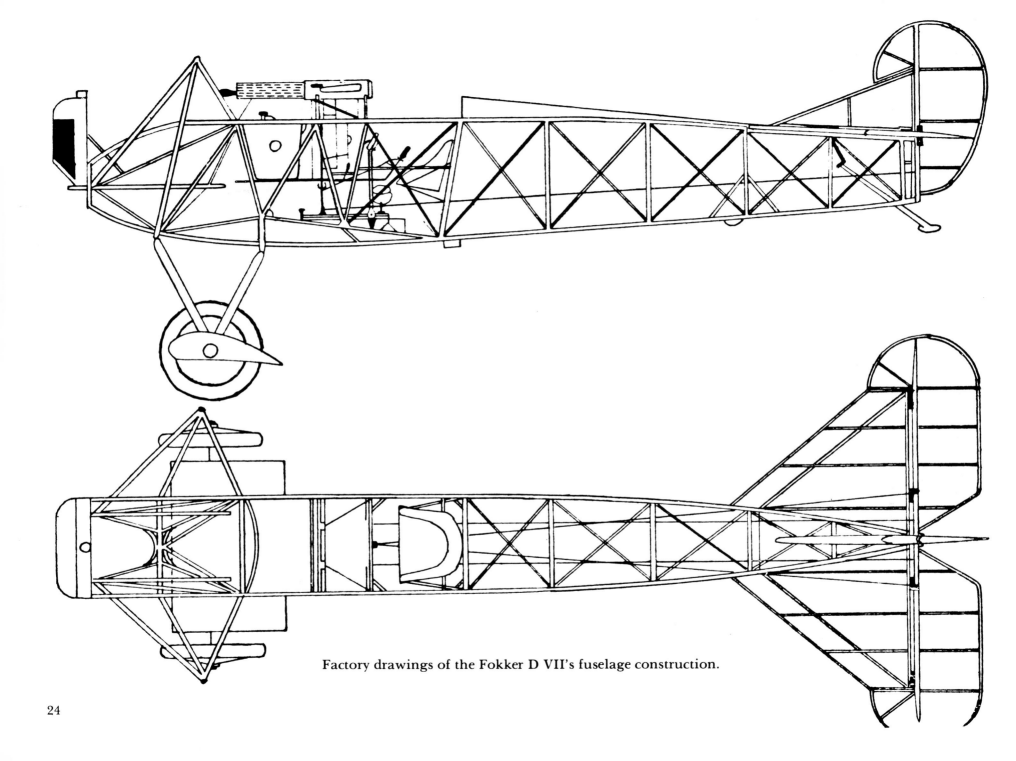

Factory drawings of the Fokker D VII's fuselage construction.

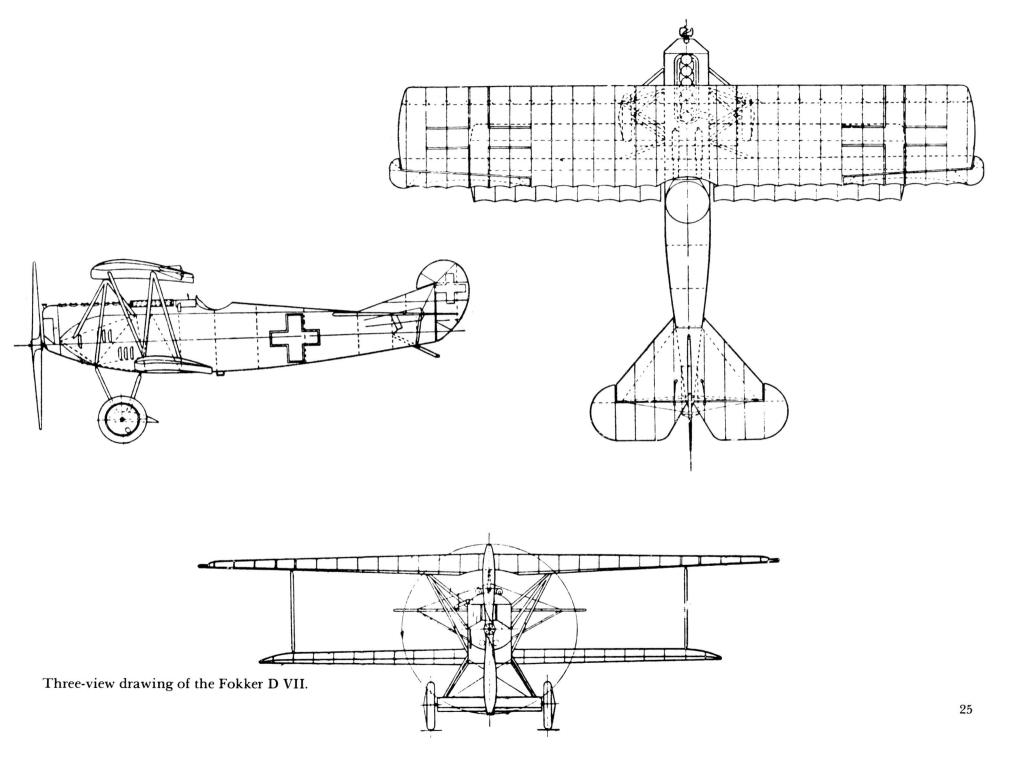

Three-view drawing of the Fokker D VII.

Mercedes DF 170, high-altitude engine for the Fokker D VII.
It carried the military designation of D IIIa.

Oberleutnant Robert Ritter von Greim, leader of the
Bavarian *Jasta* 34 with 25 aerial victories; he died on 24 May
1945 as the last commander-in-chief of the Luftwaffe.

Right: BMW III, 185hp, with which the D VII achieved the
best flight performance.

Series production of the Fokker D VII at the Albatros Works in Berlin-Johannisthal.

Albatros test pilot Richard Scholz in the Fokker D VII (Alb).

Fokker test pilot Erich Kuhlisch with a Fokker D VII F.

25000 Reichsmarks apiece. However, the greatest victory for Fokker was that Albatros, his biggest competitor, was required to build the Fokker D VII. It would not be within the scope of this book to discuss the individual qualities of the Fokker D VII. This aircraft influenced single-seat fighter design in every country for many years, since aircraft designers adhered to its basic concept well into the thirties. Germany's enemies had hoped to receive at least 2000 Fokker D VII aircraft after the war, but in actuality there were not even 1000 of them built.

Aside from the previously mentioned V.11 and V.18, Fokker also constructed two other examples of D VII aircraft in January of 1918, both of which were equipped with the 160hp Mercedes engine. V.21 differed from the standard D VII only through a different wing construction. V.22 had a four-blade propeller, which blades were arranged at 70/110 degrees to each other instead of the normal 90 degrees. This arrangement was often used on Austrian engines. It is therefore possible that V.22 was equipped with a 180hp Austro-Daimler engine. Neither the V.21 nor the V.22 were put into production.

While Fokker and Albatros were feverishly preparing for production, there were also studies being done to strengthen the wings of the triplane. For, as mentioned earlier, the triplane had to be recalled from front-line operations. JG 1, the only Geschwader which had been operating the triplane, reverted back to flying only Albatros V and Pfalz D III aircraft in December and January. The first triplanes with strengthened wings arrived at the front during the middle of February. Older versions were also re-equipped with the new wings.

But still the triplane remained haunted by problems. On March 1, *Lt.* Mohnicke of *Jasta* 11 crashed in Dr. I/155/17, and on March 6th Lt. Bahr crashed in Dr. I/106/17. The newly established *Jagdgeschwader* 2 lost its commander, *Hauptmann* Adolf Ritter von Tutschek, on March 15th, 1918, while he was flying Dr. I/404/17. In the meantime, Manfred von Richthofen again began flying triplanes. On March 18th, while flying Dr. I/152/17, he scored his 66th aerial victory. Beginning the middle of April he flew Dr. I/425/17, in which he scored his 80th and final kill on April 20.

On 21 April, 1918 he failed to return from an enemy patrol. To this day, the controversy surrounding the circumstances of his death continues. While there are many who, like the author, maintain that he was shot down in the normal fashion, there are others, such as Vice Air Marshal Collishaw (Canada), who claim that Richthofen was forced to make an emergency landing behind enemy lines where he was machine-gunned by ground troops.

Shortly after Richthofen's death the first Fokker D VII aircraft arrived at the front, initially going again to *JG* 1. Both the successor of Tutschek at *JG* 2, *Hauptmann* Berthold, and the commander of the new *JG* 3, *Hauptmann* Bruno Loerzer, received brand new D VII aircraft. V.24, a test example with a 220hp Benz engine, was not put into production since the BMW 185hp had now become available and the D VII's performance was at an optimum with this engine. In the meantime, series production was going at full steam.

Albatros had suffered a few difficulties. When Willi Hackenberger, the engineer responsible for duplication, showed up at

Factory fresh Fokker D VII (Alb) 541/18 in front of the assembly hangar.

Factory fresh Fokker D VII (OAW) 6376/18 in front of the hangar in Schneidemühl.

Fokker D VII with 185hp BMW III, recognizable due to its exhaust supports.

Fokker D VII (Alb) with a 160hp Mercedes D IIIa, with modified exhaust supports.

Fokker in Schwerin-Görries to get the blueprints, it was found that they simply didn't exist. Fokker's chief designer, Reinhold Platz, had never had drawings made up; instead, sketches were done for each aircraft design on graph paper to a scale of 1:100. In practice, the basic dimensions used for cutting were transferred directly onto the construction material by making chalk drawings on the walls and floors and then taking measurements using a yardstick. Hackenberger therefore requested the delivery of two D VII examples, which Albatros then used to make the first blueprints for the Fokker D VII! In July of 1918 there were already 407 D VII aircraft at the front, in September — 828. By the end of the War there were still 775 Fokker D VII aircraft, operating with 43 *Jagdstaffeln*. All Knights of the "Pour le Mérite" who received this high honor while as a fighter pilot flew the D VII. An English aviation historian put it best: "the D VII made aces out of beginners!" In actuality, the D VII was so easy to fly that it could be placed in the hands of beginners, who could then be sent to the front after a short period of training. An example of this is Willi Gabriel, then a *Vicefeldwebel* and later a *Hauptmann* with the Luftwaffe; he was transferred from *Schlachtstaffel* 15 (two-seater) to *Jasta* 11 on May 15th. On May 19, he had already scored his second victory, his first being credited while with *Schlachtstaffel* 15. On July 18, he shot down three single-seat enemy fighters and a bomber while on a solo flight.

But even the D VII had its pitfalls, which weren't due to design but to poor workmanship in construction. On July 15th, 1918, *Lt.* Friedrichs of Jasta 10 burned to death in Fokker D VII 309/18. The aircraft had burst

The wreckage of *Lt*. Friedrich's aircraft of *Jasta* 10, seen in Cappy in April of 1918. Notice the different cross designs on the wing and other parts of the aircraft.

Jagdstaffel 71; in the foreground is the aircraft of *Staffel* leader *Lt*. Menkhoff.

Lothar von Richthofen in front of his Fokker D VII 244/18.

The crash of *Unteroffizier* Bruder of *Jasta* 84 (12 victories).

Fokker D VII, probably that of *Oberleutnant* Auffahrt of *Jasta* 29.

On the left is an Austrian-built MAG triplane and to the right is a D VII with a 160hp Mercedes engine.

A Fokker D VII with a 185hp BMW of an unidentified *Jagdstaffel*.

Oblt. Rudolf Berthold, leader of *JG* 2 (44 victories). He was beaten to death by communists on 15 March 1920 in Harburg.

Lt. Rudolf Stark, leader of *Jasta* 35, in a Fokker D VII (OAW).

Lt. Arthur Laumann, the last leader of *Jasta* 10 (26 victories). Notice the telescopic gunsight.

Lt. Ulrich Neckel was the last leader of *Jasta* 6 (30 victories). He died on May 11th, 1928.

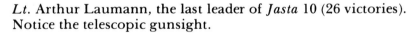

Oblt. Harald Auffahrt, the final leader of *Jasta* 29, had 26 aerial victories.

Vicefeldwebel Oscar Hennrich of *Jasta* 46 (18 victories).

Oblt. Otto Schmidt, the final leader of *Jasta* 5 (24 victories).

Lt. Emil Thuy, *Jasta* 28 (32 victories). He was killed in a crash while flying near Smolensk on 11 June 1930.

Lt. Ernst Udet, who later became the *Generalluftzeugmeister* of the Luftwaffe, was the leader of *Jasta* 4. His 62 kills made him the most successful fighter pilot of the First World War after Richthofen. Here he poses in front of his Fokker D VII in Darmstadt shortly before handing it over to the victors.

The damaged Fokker D VII of the commander of *Jagdgeschwader* 3, *Hauptmann* Bruno Lörzer, who was the leader of II *Fliegerkorps* in the Second World War.

Lt. Beckmann, leader of *Jasta* 56 (7 victories). He was known in the Second World War as the leader of KGr.zbV 500, based near Demyansk.

Lt. Riedel, *Jasta* 19, which was a part of *Jagdgeschwader* 2.

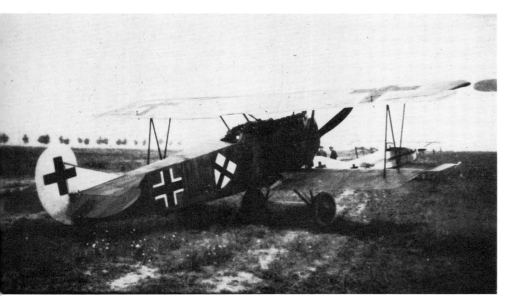

Leutnant Kraut's Fokker D VII of *Jasta* 4. The aircraft carried the symbol of the pilot's home town, the city of Thorn in West Prussia.

Hermann Göring, the leader of *Jagdgeschwader* 1 (22 victories), seen in his white Fokker D VII.

A Fokker D VII of a naval *Jagdstaffel* in Flanders.

Another D VII of the naval *Jagdgeschwader*.

A Fokker D VII of the Sachsenberg *Geschwader* seen in Swinemünde in 1919.

Fokker D VII 332/18 of an unknown *Jagdstaffel*.

This photo of a German *Jagdstaffel,* taken in the fall of 1918, particularly demonstrates the shortage of aircraft; in the foreground is a Fokker D VII, followed by an Albatros D Va, another D VII, and two triplanes.

The Fokker V.34, a modification of the V.24, with a 185hp BMW, seen in the summer of 1918.

Udet in the Fokker V.35, a two-seater with a 185hp BMW, during the summer of 1918.

The Fokker V.36, similar to the D VII but with a reduced wingspan. During trials it proved to be superior to the D VII but was never put into production.

The Fokker V.38, an enlarged two-seat fighter version of the D VII. It was only an experimental design, with a 185hp BMW.

into flames while in flight without any enemy contact. The next day, the same thing happened to *Leutnant* Bender's D VII/2063/18 of *Jasta* 4, and with another D VII of *Jasta* 45. The reason for the accidents: as a result of the extreme heat in the Fokker D VII, which did not have sufficient ventilation, the pressurized fuel expanded drastically. Since the fuel tanks had often been criticized for being of poor workmanship, and easily sprang leaks, the issuing fuel ignited upon coming in contact with the phosphorus ammunition in the machine gun belts. The required changes were immediately undertaken by the troops, and recommendations were passed on to the manufacturer by the Inspection der Fliegertruppe (IdFlieg). Fokker constructed four other experimental aircraft in 1918, V.33 to V.36, but in spite of several improvements these, too, were not put into production.

Following the cease-fire, all Fokker D VII were handed over. That these aircraft were so important can be ascertained from the fact that the cease-fire terms specifically proscribed that these aircraft be turned over. After the war, the D VII was flown in military service by the USA, Switzerland, and Poland. A few D VII aircraft in the USA had the title role in several aviation films. In 1933 Alfred Friedrich, an Alter Adler, had two Fokker triplanes and two D VII aircraft replicated in Straussberg bei Berlin. These were flown in the films "D III 88" and "Pour le Mérite." One of the two triplanes was displayed in the Lehrter Bahnhof aviation collection in Berlin, where it became a victim of a bombing raid in the Second World War. Two D VII aircraft and a reduced-scale triplane replica are still flying in the USA today. As a final note, it should be mentioned that Richard

Dietrich, a pre-war flyer from Mannheim, designed a smaller version of the D VII with a Siemens Sternmotor. This became the best training and aerobatic aircraft of the post-war period.

Technical Data

	Dr. 1	D VII	D VII/V.15
Powerplant	Le Rhone	Mercedes D III	BMW IIIa
Performance in h/p	110	160	185
Width in meters	6.73	8.9	8.9
Length in meters	5.75	6.95	6.95
Height in meters	2.73	2.75	2.75
Wing area in sq.m.	16	20.5	20.5
Empty Wt. in kg.	370	700	715
Cargo Wt. in kg.	200	180	180
Flight wt. in kg.	570	880	895
Maximum speed in kph	160	189	200
Time to 1000m in min.	–	4:15	1:4
Time to 3000m in min.	–	8:18	6:00
Time to 4000m in min.	10:00	–	–
Ceiling in meters	5000	5000	6000
Range in km.	300	350	350

Armament (same for all aircraft) 2 LMG 08/15

Experimental D VII with a wood fuselage design, instead of the tubular steel framing.

A D VII which fell intact into the hands of the Americans.

A Fokker D VII with a 160hp Mercedes D IIIa.

A scene from the 1933 film "Pour le Mérite" showing a reproduction of a D VII.

Delivered Fokker D VII aircraft under French guard. *Staffel* markings were a checkerboard pattern.

Fokker D VII (OAW) 2009/18 during testing in France in 1919.

A few Fokker D VII aircraft still flew in Switzerland after 1918.

Even the Poles acquired a few Fokker D VII, which were then flown by Polish units.

A large number of Fokker D VII aircraft were shipped to the United States and were primarily flown out of McCook Field.

Fokker D VII 7776/18 at McCook Field.

An American modification of a D VII with a Packard engine.

A Fokker D VII with a Hall-Scott L 6 engine.

Fokker D VII 7745/18 of the Tallman-Mantz collection in California. This aircraft is still flying today with a Hispano-Suiza engine.

A Fokker D VII, which Fokker took with him when he left Germany in 1918 and sold to the Dutch air force.

Munich-Oberwiesenfeld in October of 1919, where Udet and Ritter von Greim conducted demonstration flights. Greim is at the controls and Udet is standing on the wheel.

This Fokker triplane reproduction was a part of the German aviation collection and was destroyed by American bombs.

The Dietrich DP IIa, a smaller copy of the D VII, was often seen performing mock dogfights at airshows in the 1920s.

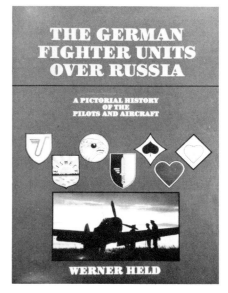
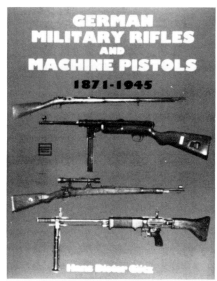